EXOTIC TEXTILES IN NEEDLEPOINT

DESIGNS FROM AROUND THE WORLD

STELLA KNIGHT

Guild of Master Craftsman Publications Ltd

First published 2003 by
Guild of Master Craftsman Publications Ltd,
166 High Street, Lewes,
East Sussex, BN7 1XN

With thanks to Lewes Town Hall, for kindly allowing us to use the location for our photography
shoot, and to Kilim, 151 High Street, Lewes, for the loan of accessories for the shoot.

Please note: thread colour codes refer to the threads used in the projects as shown in the
photographs. The charts and keys should be regarded as reference only.
Threads used in this book are supplied by Anchor, a subsidiary of Coats. Thread colour
codes therefore refer to Anchor/Coats threads only.

ISBN 1 86108 287 8

A catalogue record of this book is available from the British Library.
Publisher: Paul Richardson
Art Director: Ian Smith
Production Manager: Stuart Poole
Managing Editor: Gerrie Purcell
Commissioning Editor: April McCroskie
Editor: Clare Miller
Designer: John Hawkins

Typeface: Sabon

Colour origination by PT Repro Multi Warna
Printed and bound by Kyodo in Singapore

EXOTIC TEXTILES IN NEEDLEPOINT

DESIGNS FROM AROUND THE WORLD

Dedication

For Andrew, Alexander and Emily.

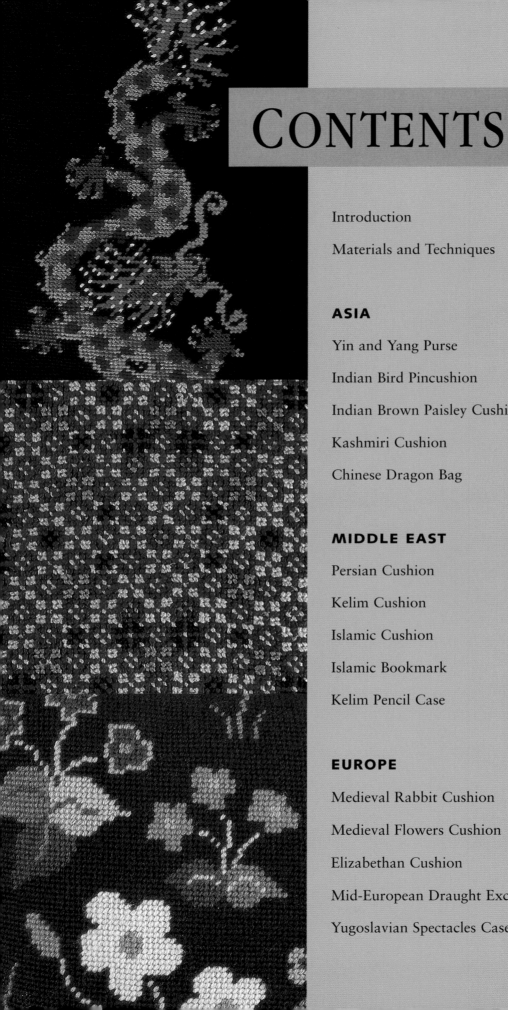

CONTENTS

INTRODUCTION

Natural fibres have been used for thousands of years to produce yarn and, ultimately, textiles. Textiles made from linen thread have been found in some ancient Egyptian tombs, and the first cotton cloth is believed to have been woven in India. The Chinese were producing silk before the birth of Christ, and the actual process of obtaining this yarn was a closely guarded secret for many years. All these yarns were developed from man's early experiments in utilizing the natural sources of fibres around him.

The word 'textiles' refers to all fabrics, especially those that are woven. Each fabric has its own characteristics that depend upon the kind of raw materials used, the structure of the cloth and the addition of any decoration produced by printing or dyeing.

The range of fibres is limited as only a certain number of animal and vegetable fibres are suitable for producing yarns. The main factors governing this are flexibility, fineness, and a high ratio of length to thickness. Each fibre has its own characteristic appearance and its own special quality, for which it is used accordingly.

Different cultures from around the world have developed their own distinct designs from the resources available to them. Oriental carpet weaving originated in Central Asia more than

2000 years ago among nomadic Turkic-speaking peoples. These tribes moved westward across the Steppes of Russia and through Persia into Caucasus and Anatolia (Asian Turkey), finally reaching the shores of the Aegean Sea around the eleventh century. Their weaving skills were spread throughout the area and patterns were constantly repeated over the centuries, being mainly derived from the decorative Islamic Kufic script.

These strong distinct designs are very different to the textiles produced in Europe, and within Europe different styles were characteristic of different countries. They all, however, valued the art of the embroiderer. In Norway, beautifully embroidered cloths were used to cover the bread that guests traditionally brought with them to feasts. In the Minho region in Portugal typical peasant needlework was the 'sweetheart handkerchief', which young girls embroidered to give to the man of their choice. In Finland, the embroidery on the bridegroom's shirt was the customary way of demonstrating the sewing skills of the bride.

The social class of embroiderers who have worked as amateurs or professionals over the centuries has ranged from members of European royal families to the humblest peasant woman. Mary, Queen of Scots, worked on numerous embroidery projects during her long captivity, while the milkmaids in eighteenth-century Denmark often spent the long winter evenings spinning and producing needlework of outstanding quality.

Perhaps surprisingly, the contribution made by men to the art of needlework has been considerable – though their role tended to be that of the chief designer rather than of the artisan. During the Middle Ages, the majority of professional embroiderers were male with women working for them. In Poland, where there was a strong tradition of gold and pearl embroidery, such work was done by men while women worked on finer embroideries and linen. As early as the thirteenth century in France, there was a guild system for embroiderers, which included both men and women. Strong family traditions were maintained because sons and sons-in-law of master broiderers were favoured.

The volume of needlework produced in a country can also be a reflection on the type of life being led at that time. The early pioneers in North America struggled hard on the land and had little time for leisure activities like needlework. However, by the second half of the eighteenth century, the demands of early colonial life had been replaced by a less strenuous existence so more time was available for needlework and experimentation with sophisticated designs and techniques. Even so, the country was still not rich, so the smallest pieces of fabric were saved for quilts, while worn sheets and blankets were used as linings and interlinings.

In recent years needlepoint has enjoyed a huge revival in popularity and there is a wide and ever-increasing range of designs and projects to make. In this book I have tried to take some of the more well-known textile designs and recreate them in needlepoint. The book has been divided into five regional chapters – Asia, -Middle East, Europe, Africa, and North and South America – and characteristic aspects of each have been depicted in needlepoint. I hope you enjoy recreating a selection of the designs in these pages and adding your own personal touch to each.

MATERIALS AND TECHNIQUES

Needlepoint is a form of canvas work embroidery in which the stitches entirely cover the material on which the work is done. Various stitches can be included under the term 'canvas work embroidery' but needlepoint generally implies using a half cross stitch or tent stitch.

It is very important to work in good light and to try to keep the tension of the threads the same throughout to give a professional finish. This technique either comes naturally right from the beginning or may take you a while to perfect. Practise several rows of stitches on small pieces of canvas and try to keep the tension the same all the way through. Do not pull the yarn too tightly as the thread will not cover the holes and the canvas may begin to twist.

Materials

CANVAS

The material on which needlepoint is worked is called canvas. It is made in two different forms; a plain canvas woven of single threads, which I call interlock canvas, and a double-thread canvas that, as the name implies, has two rows of threads lying in pairs. Both are made in fine and coarse sizes and I have tended to keep mainly to the 12-hole to the inch canvas, with some finer projects worked on 14-hole canvas.

You can alter the designs by choosing a canvas of a different-sized mesh to that stated. For example, if one particular design used a 12-hole canvas and you would prefer the size of the project to be smaller, then use a 14-hole canvas. Alternatively, if you want to enlarge a design use a coarser canvas, remembering that a doubled yarn may be needed to cover the canvas.

FRAMES

Needlepoint can either be worked on a frame or in the hand. The finished piece will be less distorted if worked on a frame but the embroidery is much more portable when not worked on a frame. Any distortion of the work not done on a frame can be counteracted by a process known as stretching when the stitching is finished. When working in the hand it is sometimes helpful to stick masking tape around the canvas edges to stop the canvas from catching your clothes.

NEEDLES

The proper needlepoint needles are long, strong and blunt with oval eyes wide enough to be easily threaded. They can be obtained at all needlework and haberdashery shops where they are generally sold as tapestry needles. They come in a variety of sizes and I have tended to use a size 20 on the projects using 12-hole canvas and a smaller needle on the 14-hole canvas.

THREADS

For a long while wool and silk were the only materials used in needlepoint but now cotton threads have been dyed in wonderful colours and are much cheaper to buy. Silk and cotton, however, are not suitable for articles which are to be subjected to long and harsh usage as their delicate and fragile nature offers too little resistance. Wool is far more durable and when stitched over a cotton canvas the worked embroidery is extremely hard-wearing.

Any cleaning that is required can be done with a good spot upholstery dry cleaner or with a gentle wash of soapy water applied with a sponge, ensuring that the material is not soaked. If coffee or ink is spilt on the work it is important to rinse it under running cold water immediately, leave it to dry naturally and then press it. If the stain still shows it may be necessary to unpick the area and then restitch it.

After several years of wear, the embroidery may appear to be getting thin and it is then best to unpick the area and restitch it. I would advise storing a few strands of each of the yarn colours used in a project just in case restitching has to be done in later years.

Techniques

STARTING AND FINISHING

Tying a knot in the yarn end is an easy way to start but this is not the best way to work. Start by passing the needle down through the canvas about 25mm (1in) from where the first stitch is to be and leave a 100mm (4in) end. Hold this tight as you begin to stitch.

After working several stitches take the yarn end to the wrong side and secure it by passing the yarn through the backs of the worked stitches. Finish the yarn by passing it through the backs of worked stitches.

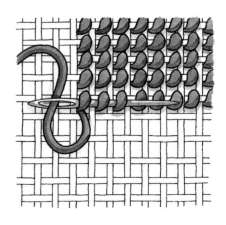

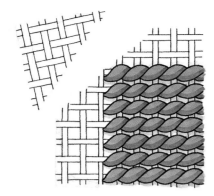

CUTTING CORNERS

After finishing the stitching for a project the corners of the canvas should be cut diagonally. This avoids a build-up of a bulk of canvas in the corners after making up, which could distort the finished work.

STRETCHING THE FINISHED NEEDLEPOINT

When the embroidery has been completed the canvas may be slightly askew. This is easily rectified by dampening it on the back with warm water, pinning it firmly to a board covered with a tea towel and allowing it to dry naturally. Be careful not to soak the needlepoint. When tugging it back into shape you can be quite firm with the embroidery and you will need to position the drawing pins about 15mm ($\frac{5}{8}$in) from each other. When dry, unpin the work, press it on the back with a hot steam iron and the design should then be ready to make up. If the work is still distorted repeat the process.

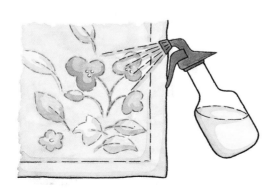

BACKING A CUSHION

Backing a cushion is a simple process either using a sewing machine or sewing by hand. The backing material you choose should be reasonably thick – I tend to use upholstery velvet which is readily available in a great variety of colours. You can use zips for attaching the opening and they will allow the cushion pad to be removed easily. Alternatively, you can leave a gap at the bottom of a cushion, stitching it up after the cushion pad has been inserted.

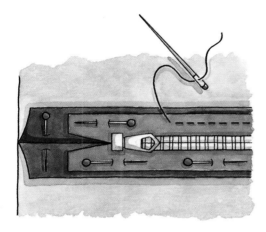

When inserting a zip fastener you will need to cut two pieces of fabric. To calculate the size divide the area of the stretched needlepoint in half widthwise and add about 15mm (⅝in) seam allowance all round to each piece. With right sides together join at each end of the centre seam, leaving enough seam open in the middle for the length of the zip fastener. Pin and tack the zip fastener into position and stitch it using a sewing machine with a zip foot or by hand using backstitch.

A good selection of trimmings can be sewn to the edges of a cushion which can make a stunning finish.

Stitches

HALF CROSS STITCH

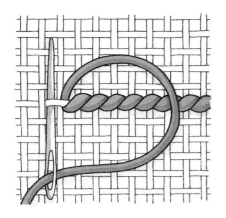

This stitch can be worked either from right to left or from left to right. It is important to ensure that all the stitches slope in the same direction on the front of the canvas. On the back you should see short vertical stitches.

LONG-ARMED CROSS STITCH

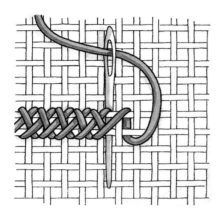

I have used this decorative stitch to join the fronts and backs of pincushions. It is similar to cross stitch but the 'crosses' are worked closer together and with a longer top stitch leaving no canvas showing. You need to work two holes forwards, and one hole back.

TENT STITCH

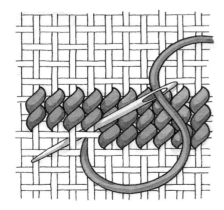

This is a more hard-wearing stitch than the half cross stitch as it completely covers the canvas on both sides. The half cross stitch only covers the face of the embroidery. However, it does use more yarn (sometimes up to a third more), which should be noted when buying materials for a design.

CROSS STITCH

This stitch forms a cross on the front of the design. Work a row of half cross stitches and then work back in the opposite direction. When mixing half cross and cross stitches in one design I make the top cross stitch run in the opposite direction to the rest of the half cross stitches for maximum effect.

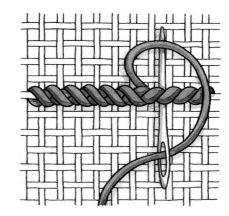

SLIP STITCH

This is a neat way to join embroidery to lining fabric, for example when making up spectacle cases or purses. It is very quick and simple to do and ensures no unworked canvas is shown. Slip stitching is also used to close open seams and is almost invisible when worked correctly.

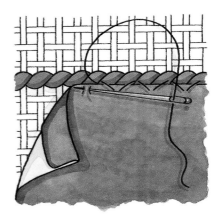

ASIA

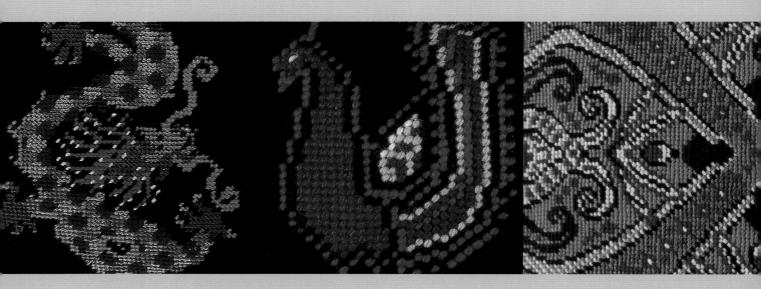

The origin of all oriental carpet weaving lies in Central Asia among the nomadic Turkic-speaking peoples of more than 2000 years ago. The westward movement of these tribes began with their travels across the Steppes of Russia and through Persia into the Caucasus and Anatolia, until they finally reached the shores of the Aegean Sea around the eleventh century. Most of the oriental carpets that have been coming to Western Europe for the last 500 years were woven in Anatolia in villages close to the Aegean seaboard. They were probably shipped from there to Venice, an important trading centre at that time, before being sent elsewhere in Europe.

The region of Central Asia was once largely populated by a number of nomadic tribes who relied upon their weaving skills to provide a wide range of items for their own domestic use. Much of the weaving was functional rather than decorative but some very fine items were woven for special occasions such as weddings. Tribal weaving throughout the region has been badly affected by war, famine and political upheaval, and far fewer genuine carpets are being woven in Afghanistan or Turkestan

at the present time. In their place a modern carpet industry has emerged in nearby Pakistan where many of the traditional Afghan and Turkoman designs are being made under workshop conditions.

Embroidery is one of the finest Chinese national arts and has been used for centuries by the Chinese to describe splendid or exquisite things such as, for instance, a land of incomparable beauty or a promising future or wit. The historical records of the Qin dynasty mentions things like 'embroidered robes and undergarments' and 'white robes embroidered with red designs'.

Though multicoloured figured brocade became popular in the Spring-and-Autumn and Warring States periods, it could not compare with embroidery for artistic appeal and this was particularly true where large-scale designs were concerned. Moreover, there was still a premium on clothes with designs either painted or embroidered on them, owing to the difficulty of the techniques involved in their making and the restrictions of tradition.

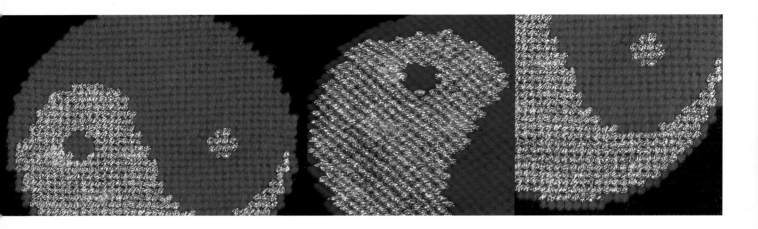

YIN AND YANG PURSE

MATERIALS

- 1 skein each of tapisserie wool 9800, 8216
- 1 reel gold Kreinik Heavy Braid 002
- 1 piece 12-hole interlock canvas size 203mm (8in) square
- Backing fabric – I have used black velvet
- 2 pieces of lining fabric
- 1 popper

This is a simple easy-to-stitch design based on the Yin and Yang symbol found in the teachings of Lao Zi who founded Taoism. He lived at the same time as Confucius in the fifth century BC and in his lifetime he described how to live at peace and in balance with nature. He called these balances between opposite forces 'Yin and Yang'. I have used the symbol here to make a little purse that would be ideal for use in the evening.

Instructions

1 Follow the chart to work the design, starting from the middle. Use half cross stitch throughout.

2 Press the embroidery on the back with a hot steam iron over a damp cloth and gently pull it back into shape.

3 Trim any excess canvas to within 13mm (½in) and cut the corners diagonally.

4 With wrong sides together, slip stitch one piece of lining fabric to the embroidered piece.

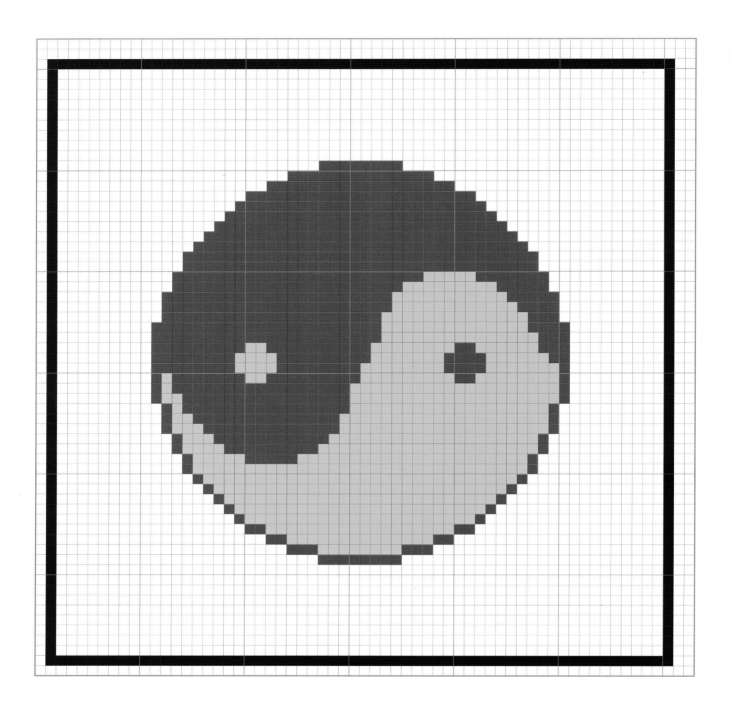

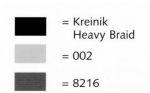

■	= Kreinik Heavy Braid
▨	= 002
▨	= 8216

5 Do the same with the backing fabric and the other piece of lining fabric.

6 Stitch the two pieces together.

7 Carefully oversew the seams on the outside with the gold thread.

INDIAN BIRD PINCUSHION

MATERIALS

- 1 skein each of tapisserie wool 8691, 8136, 8218, 8990, 8006, 9800
- 2 pieces 12-hole interlock canvas size 152mm (6in) square
- Stuffing

This little motif has been taken from a nineteenth-century skirt fragment from the Gujarat region of India. It was originally produced on semi-transparent silk fabrics using a high proportion of gold and silver threads. The designs are transferred to the fabric by the 'prick-and-pounce' method using a powder mixture which is put onto a cloth pad and pressed through a strong paper on which the design has been drawn and pricked.

Instructions

1. Follow the chart to work the design, starting from the middle. Use half cross stitch throughout.
2. Press the embroideries on the back with a hot steam iron over a damp cloth and gently pull back into shape.

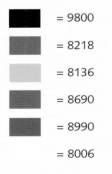

■	= 9800
■	= 8218
■	= 8136
■	= 8690
■	= 8990
	= 8006

3 Trim any excess canvas to within 13mm (½in) and cut the corners diagonally.

4 With wrong sides facing, sew the two pieces together with a long-armed cross stitch. Leave a 51mm (2in) gap.

5 Stuff the pincushion.

6 Sew up the gap.

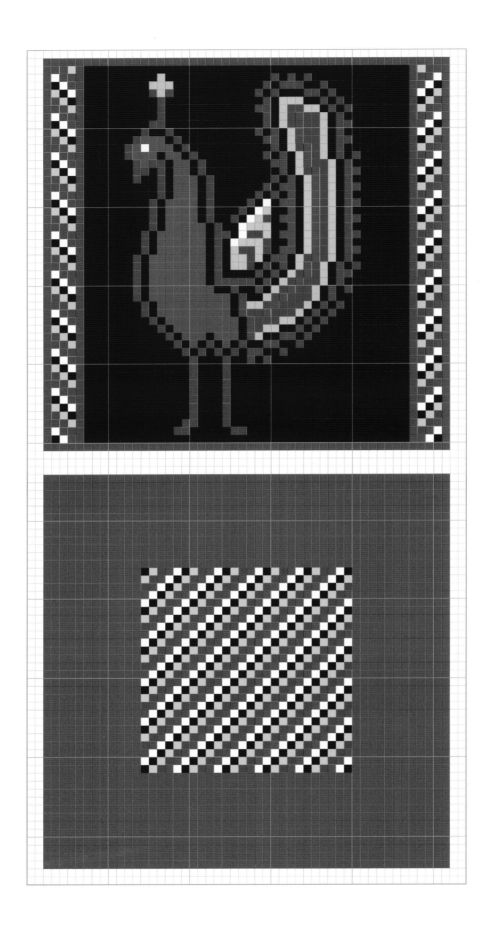

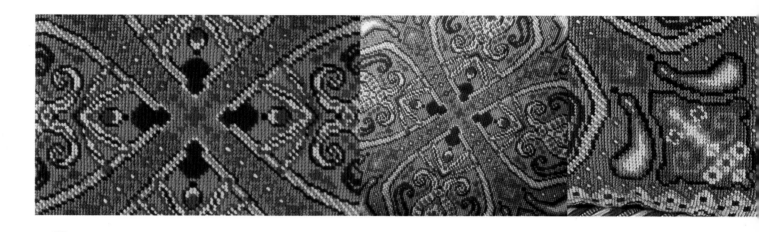

INDIAN BROWN PAISLEY CUSHION

MATERIALS
- 1 skein tapisserie wool 9362
- 2 skeins tapisserie wool 8240, 9658, 3124, 8252
- 4 skeins tapisserie wool 9646, 8354
- 6 skeins tapisserie 9510
- 1 piece 12-hole interlock canvas size 508mm (20in) square
- Dark red velvet backing fabric
- Cushion pad size 450mm (17¾in) square
- 2m trimmings

This design is one of the classic Indian motifs – the paisley – and originally comes from Kashmir. Traditionally it is thought that this type of embroidery developed when the menders of woven shawls, who repaired worn parts by joining pieces invisibly, were asked to hand-stitch the entire shawl. The stitchers made motifs, borders and, ultimately, a fabric of solid stitching; that is, with no background fabric showing.

Instructions

1 Follow the chart to work the design, starting from the middle. Use half cross-stitch throughout.

2 Press the embroidery on the back with a hot steam iron over a damp cloth and gently pull it back into shape. If it is still not straight dampen it again, pin it to a wooden board covered with a tea towel and leave to dry.

■	= 8354
■	= 9620
■	= 9646
□	= 9362
■	= 9510
□	= 8252
■	= 8240
■	= 9658

3 With right sides together, sew the backing fabric to the embroidery on three sides.

4 Trim any excess canvas to within 13mm (½in) and cut the corners diagonally.

5 Turn right sides out and insert the cushion pad.

6 Close the open seam with slip stitch.

7 Sew on trimmings.

KASHMIRI CUSHION

MATERIALS

- 3 skeins tapisserie wool 9362,
- 4 skeins tapisserie wool 8100, 8692, 9788
- 5 skeins tapisserie wool 8542, 8404
- 1 piece 12-hole interlock canvas size 508mm (20in) square
- Dark red velvet backing fabric
- Cushion pad 450mm (17¾in) square
- 2m trimmings

Similar to the Paisley Cushion, this design was created by the woven-and-embroidered-shawl technique developed at the end of the nineteenth century. The embroidery could be stitched so that the shawl was double-sided, or stitched through just half of the fabric so that the design was seen only on one side with nothing showing on the reverse. Very fine stitches were used and few old pieces survive.

Instructions

1. Follow the chart to work the design, starting from the middle. Use half cross stitch throughout.

2. Press the embroidery on the back with a hot steam iron over a damp cloth and gently pull it back into shape. If it is still not straight, dampen it again, pin it to a wooden board covered with a tea towel and leave to dry.

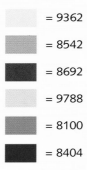

▫	= 9362
▨	= 8542
▦	= 8692
▫	= 9788
▩	= 8100
▦	= 8404

3 With right sides together, sew the backing fabric to the embroidery on three sides.

4 Trim any excess canvas and fabric to within 13mm (½in). Also cut the corners diagonally.

5 Turn right sides out and insert the cushion pad.

6 Close the open seam with slip stitch.

7 Sew on trimmings.

CHINESE DRAGON BAG

MATERIALS

- 1 skein each of stranded cotton 47, 57, 175, 146, 134, 333, 100, 290, 187
- 4 skeins stranded cotton 403
- 1 piece of 14-hole interlock canvas size 203mm x 279mm (8in x 11in)
- Black velvet backing fabric
- 2 pieces of red velvet fabric size 254mm x 127mm (10in x 5in)
- Lining fabric
- Gold-beaded braid 381mm (15in) long
- Thick braid for handle approximately 1422mm (56in) long

The Lunar New Year is the most important festival of the Chinese year. It is the celebration to welcome the start of a new year and a festival of family reunion. In ancient China the dragon was considered a friendly and helpful beast and was associated with long life, good fortune and rain. Dragon dances are the most spectacular dances performed at New Year and dragon designs are seen in all manner of everyday life including textiles.

Instructions

1 Follow the chart to work the design, starting from the middle. Use half cross stitch throughout.

2 Press the embroidery on the back with a hot steam iron over a damp cloth and gently pull it back into shape.

3 Trim any excess canvas to within 13mm (½in) and cut the corners diagonally.

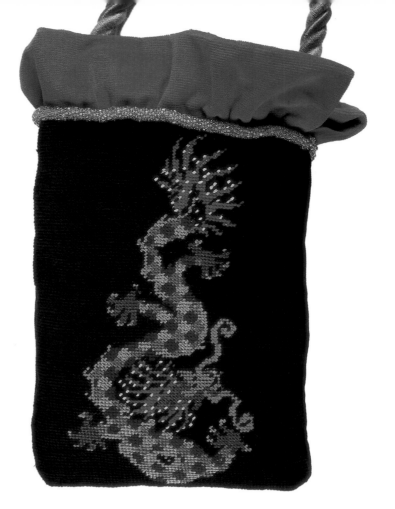

▨	= 291
▨	= 329
▨	= 27
▧	= 403
▨	= 109
▨	= 186
▨	= 130
▨	= 131
▨	= 133
▨	= 1098

4 Fold the red velvet pieces in half, right sides outermost, and stitch one piece to the back of the embroidery and one piece to the wrong side of the backing fabric. Loosely pleat the fabric to draw it in, making it the same size as the main embroidery.

5 Attach the thick braid to the inside of the bag to be used as a handle.

6 Cut two pieces of lining fabric to the same size as the embroidery. Sew together on three sides leaving the top edge open.

7 Slip the lining into the case. Turn the top edges in and slip stitch together neatly.

8 Finally, carefully sew the gold braid around the top edge of the bag.

MIDDLE EAST

The outstanding richness of Islamic art lies in the complex use of geometrical pattern. It is evident that many of these patterns have their origin in the cultures that once dominated these lands – Greek, Roman, Byzantine, Central Asian and Persian – but the Islamic craftsmen soon developed a distinctive style and have, over the years, discovered and devised ever more complex patterned schemes.

The buildings of the Islamic world are a delight of geometry, with ingenious patterns covering the walls, ceilings, floors and windows, and also much of the furniture within the rooms.

The best weaving in the Middle East occurred in the Caucasus from the nineteenth century. Many of the designs and motifs used are derived from Persian weaving although they became distorted as time passed. During the twentieth century, under Soviet influence, much of the weaving was concentrated in workshops and collectives and the earlier free designs became stilted and less attractive.

The basic design of many Turkish weavings is that of a prayer rug with an arch at one end. During the seventeenth century, many small rugs rather like double-ended prayer rugs were exported to Europe and many survive in Protestant churches in Transylvania, now part of Romania.

PERSIAN CUSHION

MATERIALS

- 6 skeins tapisserie wool 9682
- 9 skeins tapisserie wool 9800
- 10 skeins tapisserie wool 9504 and 8264
- 1 piece 12-hole interlock canvas size 508mm (20in) square
- Brown velvet backing fabric
- Cushion pad size 450mm (17¾in) square

The complex geometric patterns used in Middle Eastern designs make them rich and striking. These have evolved from designs introduced from a wide variety of conquering peoples that have gradually changed and diversified over the years. Carpet weaving in particular has been carried out in the region for many centuries and although each weaving area has its own distinctive patterns, common characteristics include the use of bold primary colours and straight lines to outline the various features of the pattern.

Instructions

1. Follow the chart to work the design, starting from the middle. Use half cross stitch throughout.

2. Press the embroidery on the back with a hot steam iron over a damp cloth and gently pull it back into shape. If it is still not straight dampen it again, pin it to a wooden board covered with a tea towel and leave to dry.

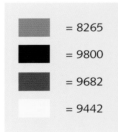

▨	= 8265
■	= 9800
▨	= 9682
□	= 9442

3 With right sides together, sew the backing fabric to the embroidery on three sides.

4 Trim any excess canvas and fabric to within 13mm (½in) and cut the corners diagonally.

5 Turn right sides out and insert the cushion pad.

6 Close the open seam with slip stitch.

7 Sew on trimmings.

Kelim Cushion

MATERIALS

- 1 skein of tapisserie wool 8690
- 4 skeins of tapisserie wool 8218, 8136
- 6 skeins of tapisserie wool 9800
- 8 skeins of tapisserie wool 8036
- 1 piece 12-hole interlock canvas size 508mm (20in) square
- Red velvet backing fabric
- Cushion pad 450mm (17¾in) square
- 2m trimmings

This design was inspired by some of the motifs found in Turkish carpets. Most were woven in villages close to the Aegean coast during the fifteenth and sixteenth centuries and began to be shipped off to Venice, then an important trading centre, before arriving in Western Europe. Carpet weaving still continues in Turkey today, though more as a cottage industry in those villages that have a centuries-old tradition in weaving. Natural vegetable dyes have even been reintroduced for use on the yarns.

Instructions

1 Follow the chart to work the design, starting from the middle. Use half cross stitch throughout.

2 Press the embroidery on the back with a hot steam iron over a damp cloth and gently pull it back into shape. If it is still not straight dampen it again, pin it to a wooden board covered with a tea towel and leave to dry.

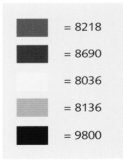

= 8218
= 8690
= 8036
= 8136
= 9800

3 Trim any excess canvas to within 13mm (½in) and cut the corners diagonally.

4 Place the embroidery and velvet backing together, right sides facing, and stitch together on three sides.

5 Insert the cushion pad and close the fourth side with slip stitches.

6 Sew on trimmings.

ISLAMIC CUSHION

MATERIALS

- 1 skein stranded cotton 45
- 2 skeins stranded cotton 363
- 3 skeins stranded cotton 188 and 160
- 4 skeins stranded cotton 2
- 7 skeins stranded cotton 137
- 1 piece 14-hole interlock canvas size 356mm (14in) square
- Red velvet backing fabric
- Stuffing
- 1m tassel trimmings

The richness of Islamic art stems from the inspiring use of geometrical pattern. Many of these patterns appear to have their origin in the cultures that once dominated these lands but the Islamic craftsmen soon developed a distinctive style and have, over the years, created and developed ever more complex patterned schemes. To capture the lightness of these complicated designs I have used stranded cotton instead of wool.

Instructions

1 Follow the chart to work the design, starting from the middle. Use half cross stitch throughout.

2 Press the embroidery on the back with a hot steam iron over a damp cloth and gently pull it back into shape. If it is still not straight dampen it again, pin it to a wooden board covered with a tea towel and leave to dry.

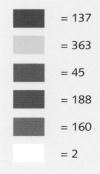

■	= 137
■	= 363
■	= 45
■	= 188
■	= 160
□	= 2

3 Trim any excess canvas to within 13mm (½in) and cut the corners diagonally.

4 Fold back the unworked canvas and carefully sew the trimming onto the back of the embroidery.

5 With wrong sides facing, sew the velvet backing to the embroidery leaving a 152mm (6in) gap along one side.

6 Fill the cushion with the stuffing and neatly sew up the gap.

ISLAMIC BOOKMARK

MATERIALS

- 1 skein each of stranded cotton 186, 2, 48, blue
- 1 piece 14-hole interlock canvas size 102mm x 254mm (4in x 10in)
- Backing fabric
- Thin cardboard
- Tassel

This, similar to the Islamic Cushion, is based on one of the fantastic array of complex geometric shapes found in Islamic art. I have taken the eight-pointed star which is a common element found and could be made more and more intricate if you wanted to expand this small design into a cushion, for example. Also, as with the Islamic Cushion, I have used stranded cotton which has a lighter more reflective feel.

Instructions

1 Follow the chart to work the design, starting from the middle. Use half cross stitch throughout.

2 Press the embroidery on the back with a hot steam iron over a damp cloth and gently pull it back into shape.

3 Trim any excess canvas to within 13mm (½in) and cut the corners at the top of the bookmark diagonally.

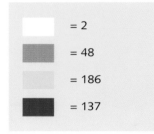

	= 2
	= 48
	= 186
	= 137

4 Cut a piece of thin cardboard to a shape slightly
smaller than the finished embroidery and attach it by
lacing together the unworked canvas tightly with
cotton thread. This is a bit fiddly but it is important
to get the work absolutely straight on the front.

5 Carefully slip stitch the backing fabric to the
embroidery and sew on the trimming.

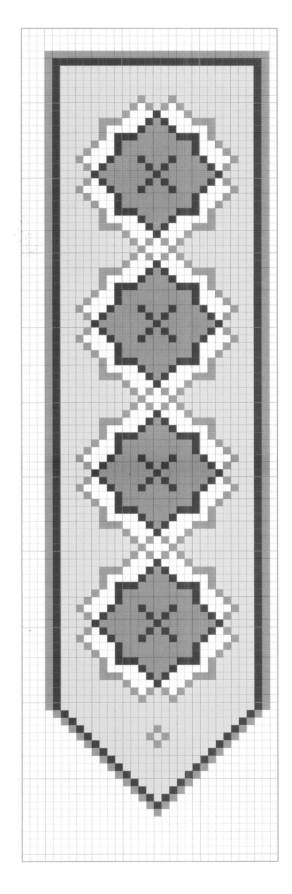

KELIM PENCIL CASE

MATERIALS

- 1 skein tapisserie wool 8490, 8006, 9646
- 2 skeins tapisserie wool 8218, 8690, 8136, 8396
- 1 piece 12-hole interlock canvas size 381mm x 254mm (15in x 10in)
- Dark red velvet fabric size 305mm x 229mm (12in x 9in)
- Lining fabric
- 305mm (12in) beaded fringe

The Caucasus Mountains and surrounding area are home to a number of distinct ethnic groups with their own languages and religions. Carpet weaving has been carried out in the region for many centuries and, although each weaving area has its own distinctive patterns, common characteristics include the use of bold primary colours and straight lines to outline the various features of the pattern.

Instructions

1 Follow the chart to work the design, starting from the middle. Use half cross stitch throughout.

2 Press the embroidery on the back with a hot steam iron over a damp cloth and gently pull it back into shape.

3 Trim any excess canvas to within 13mm (½in) and cut the corners diagonally.

4 Carefully sew the beaded fringe to the back of the top side of the embroidery.

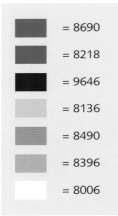

= 8690

= 8218

= 9646

= 8136

= 8490

= 8396

= 8006

5 With wrong sides together sew the lining fabric to the embroidery sewing around all four edges.

6 With right sides together sew the velvet fabric around the bottom and two side seams.

7 Fold the excess velvet fabric back on itself and slip stitch around the same seams covering all the excess fabric.

8 Turn the velvet pocket inside out.

EUROPE

'Textiles' refers to all fabrics, whether in the piece or in garment form. Fabrics are either woven or knitted and each one has its own characteristics. These depend upon the kind of raw materials used, the class of yarns, the structure of the cloth and the addition of any decoration produced by printing or dyeing. When the cloth has been determined then the embellishment in the form of embroidery can take place.

The character of European embroidery has not remained constant throughout its history and there is no continuous recognizable style. It is, however, an extremely adaptable art and can be practised by professionals of dazzling virtuosity and by amateurs who have no qualifications save a good eye and patience.

Embroidery has served a multiplicity of uses, both religious and secular, and has been an indispensable ornament of religion, of domestic furnishing and of dress. In the Christian Church, embroidery was employed from early times until the fourteenth and fifteenth centuries when embroidered altar fronts were virtually paintings made with the needle. Early English medieval embroidery was called 'opus anglicanum' and provided

some of the finest examples of English needlework. It is thought by many to transcend even the skills of illuminated manuscript painting which, during the same period, was itself reaching new heights of excellence. It became internationally famous and was much sold abroad; a Vatican inventory of 1295 lists more pieces of opus anglicanum than of any other embroidery.

Embroidery was also prominent in the home – or castle! In the vast chilly halls of the Middle Ages embroidered hangings vied with rich tapestry hangings. Beds, with their curtains and canopies, their coverlets and numerous pillows, were monuments of embroidery, particularly in the sixteenth and seventeenth centuries.

In central and south-eastern Europe the inhabitants were also prolific embroiderers. The present racial composition of the area dates mainly from the waves of nomadic migration from northern Europe and the steppes of central Asia which took place from the sixth to the tenth centuries. It was still church embroidery that was the most important, which in central Europe was either for the Roman Catholic or the Orthodox Churches.

MEDIEVAL RABBIT CUSHION

MATERIALS

- 1 skein tapisserie wool 8264, 9442, 9172, 9076, 9022, 9556, 8712
- 2 skeins tapisserie wool 9524
- 4 skeins tapisserie wool 8734
- 1 piece 12-hole interlock canvas size 457mm (18in) square
- Dark blue velvet backing fabric
- Cushion pad size 350mm (13¾in) square
- 1½m tasselled trimmings

This charming little rabbit was taken from the famous *mille fleurs* or 'thousand flowers' range of tapestries originally woven in France in the sixteenth century. In general they depict rural scenes overflowing with country freshness and charm. On these, gentle ladies, lords and peasant folk frolic on a background of 'Bord de Loire' flowers, all in muted soft-toned colours.

Instructions

1. Follow the chart to work the design, starting from the middle. Use half cross stitch throughout.

2. Press the embroidery on the back with a hot steam iron over a damp cloth and gently pull it back into shape. If it is still not straight dampen it again, pin it to a wooden board covered with a tea towel and leave to dry.

3. With right sides together, sew the backing fabric to the embroidery on three sides.

■	= 9022
■	= 9076
■	= 9172
■	= 9524
■	= 8264
■	= 8740
□	= 9442
■	= 8712
■	= 9556

4 Trim any excess canvas and fabric to within 13mm (½in). Also cut the corners diagonally.

5 Turn right sides out and insert the cushion pad.

6 Close the open seam with slip stitch.

7 Sew on trimmings.

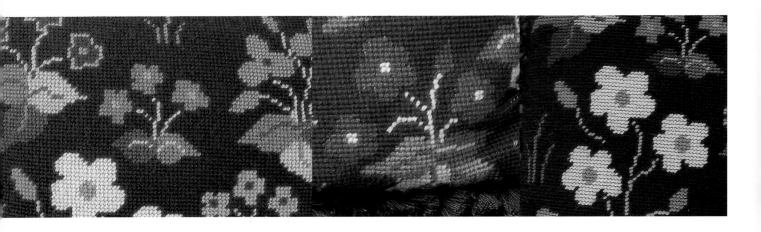

MEDIEVAL FLOWERS CUSHION

MATERIALS

- 1 skein tapisserie wool 8264, 9442, 9172, 9076, 9022, 9556, 8712, 9524
- 5 skeins tapisserie wool 8734
- 1 piece 12-hole interlock canvas size 457mm (18in) square
- Dark blue velvet backing fabric
- Cushion pad size 350mm (13¾in) square
- 1½m tasselled trimmings

In the Middle Ages early tapestries had a purely utilitarian function. They were originally designed to protect medieval rooms from damp and cold weather, to cover austere walls of big castles or to insulate big rooms into more comfortable spaces. Tapestries began to get very large in size and therefore required big looms, many workers and high capital investments. By 1500 tapestries had become a way of displaying wealth and power.

Instructions

1 Follow the chart to work the design, starting from the middle. Use half cross stitch throughout.

2 Press the embroidery on the back with a hot steam iron over a damp cloth and gently pull it back into shape. If it is still not straight, dampen it again, pin it to a wooden board covered with a tea towel and leave to dry.

■	= 9022
■	= 9076
■	= 9172
■	= 9524
■	= 8264
■	= 8740
■	= 9442
■	= 8712
■	= 9556

3 With right sides together, sew the backing fabric to the embroidery on three sides.

4 Trim any excess canvas and fabric to within 13mm (½in). Also cut the corners diagonally.

5 Turn right sides out and insert the cushion pad.

6 Close the open seam with slip stitch.

7 Sew on trimmings.

ELIZABETHAN CUSHION

MATERIALS

- 3 skeins tapisserie wool 8612, 9006, 8218
- 5 skeins tapisserie wool 8060
- 12 skeins tapisserie wool 9800
- 1 piece 12-hole interlock canvas size 457mm (18in) square
- Black velvet backing fabric
- Cushion pad size 400mm (15¾in) square
- 1½m trimmings

This design has been taken from a set of vestments traditionally thought to have been used by St Thomas of Canterbury in the twelfth century. It shows a typical formality in the repeating patterns of interlocking medallions. The original embroidery must have been a complicated and exacting process constructed to look quite natural. Technical skills displayed in later examples of this distinct style of embroidery are better examples of British needlework than at any other period.

Instructions

1 Follow the chart to work the design, starting from the middle. Use half cross stitch throughout.

2 Press the embroidery on the back with a hot steam iron over a damp cloth and gently pull it back into shape. If it is still not straight, dampen it again, pin it to a wooden board covered with a tea towel and leave to dry.

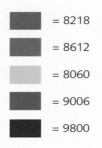

![#8218]	= 8218
![#8612]	= 8612
![#8060]	= 8060
![#9006]	= 9006
![#9800]	= 9800

3 With right sides together, sew the backing fabric to the embroidery on three sides.

4 Trim any excess canvas and fabric to within 13mm (½in). Also cut the corners diagonally.

5 Turn right sides out and insert the cushion pad.

6 Close the open seam with slip stitch.

7 Sew on trimmings.

MID-EUROPEAN DRAUGHT EXCLUDER

MATERIALS

- 4 skeins tapisserie wool 9006
- 5 skeins tapisserie wool 8006
- 6 skeins tapisserie wool 8790
- 7 skeins tapisserie wool 8218
- 40 skeins tapisserie wool 9442
- 1 piece 12-hole interlock canvas size 1118mm x 508mm (44in x 20in)
- 2 pieces red velvet size 127mm x 406mm (5in x 16in)
- 51mm x 3½mm (2in x 3½in) diameter red velvet pieces
- 51mm (2in) square cardboard pieces
- Stuffing

The motifs that I have chosen for this piece originate from central Europe – in particular, Hungary and Yugoslavia – although similarities in design can also be seen in Switzerland and Scandinavia. The designs were used in the trimmings of garments such as sheets, pillowcases and tablecloths, and were made within the home. Sometimes the designs were treated as a family secret and only displayed on festive occasions to dazzle the eyes of other villagers.

Instructions

1 Follow the chart to work the design, starting from the middle. Use half cross stitch throughout.

2 Press the embroidery on the back with a hot steam iron over a damp cloth and gently pull it back into shape. If it is still not straight dampen it again, pin it to a wooden board covered with a tea towel and leave to dry.

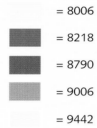

= 8006

= 8218

= 8790

= 9006

= 9442

3 Trim any excess canvas to within 13mm (½in) and cut the corners diagonally.

4 Using a long-armed cross stitch join the long seam together.

5 Sew a piece of red velvet to each end of the draught excluder. Sew up the short seam.

6 Tightly secure one end of the draught excluder by gathering together the open end.

7 Stuff the draught excluder.

8 Securely fasten up the open end of the draught excluder.

9 Cover each of the cardboard circles with the small pieces of red velvet.

10 Stitch these tightly to each end of the draught excluder.

Yugoslavian Spectacles Case

MATERIALS

- 1 skein tapisserie wool 9800, 8038, 9116, 8136, 8688, 8216
- 2 skeins tapisserie wool 8006
- 1 piece 12-hole interlock canvas size 203mm x 305mm (8in x12in)
- Dark red velvet backing fabric
- 2 pieces of lining fabric

The majority of the embroideries found in Yugoslavia and its surrounding countries are full of colour and were used for decorating garments and linen. By the age of six or seven, girls had already made their 'apprenticeship pieces' and then went on to embroider cuffs, handkerchiefs and borders for sheets and pillowcases. A young girl or woman was not thought of as a less worthy person because she could not sew well, but if she was able to embroider beautifully she may well have been able to marry above her station.

Instructions

1 Follow the chart to work the design, starting from the middle. Use half cross stitch throughout.

2 Press the embroidery on the back with a hot steam iron over a damp cloth and gently pull it back into shape.

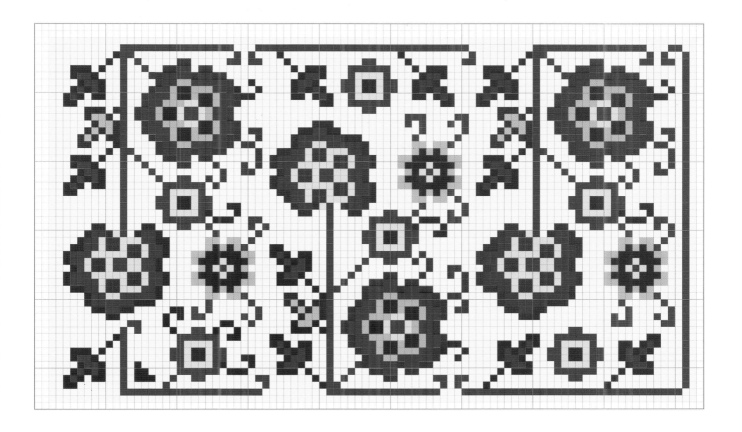

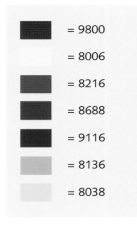

■	= 9800
□	= 8006
■	= 8216
■	= 8688
■	= 9116
■	= 8136
■	= 8038

3 Trim any excess canvas to within 13mm (½in). Also cut the corners diagonally.

4 With right sides together, sew the backing fabric to the embroidery leaving the top end open. Turn right sides out.

5 With right sides together, sew the lining fabric together leaving the top end open.

6 Put the lining inside the spectacles case and carefully sew around the open end, hiding any unworked canvas.

AFRICA

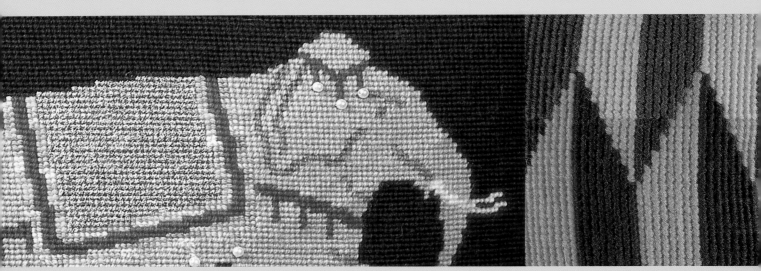

One of the most exciting things about African textiles is that there are so many ways to look at them. Cloth 'acts' in many different ways in each culture. A given piece may be both a work of art and a marker of ethnic identity. It may tell a story and also show off the owner's wealth. It may simply be a durable item of clothing with no other cultural meaning.

It is easy to see that a lot of African cloth is beautiful and well made. Weavers and dyers spend years, often from when they are young children, learning their techniques. When comparing several pieces of the same kind of cloth, similarities can be found which would denote that certain traditions were passed down through the generations. Weavers and dyers creatively use symbols,

colours and patterns to put their own unique stamp on each piece of cloth. Textile traditions are, however, always changing. Creative weavers are always coming up with new ways to make cloth in response to changes in fashion or culture. Also, contact with other cultures gives weavers and dyers new ideas and new markets for their cloth.

The cloth changes as historical circumstances change. For example, before the seventeenth century most Ashanti cloth was basically blue and white. However, with increased trade and an enriched monarchy, which could afford expensive textiles, weavers began to buy imported silk fabric and unravel it for the thread. They re-wove this into their finest cloth for the Asantehene or royal family.

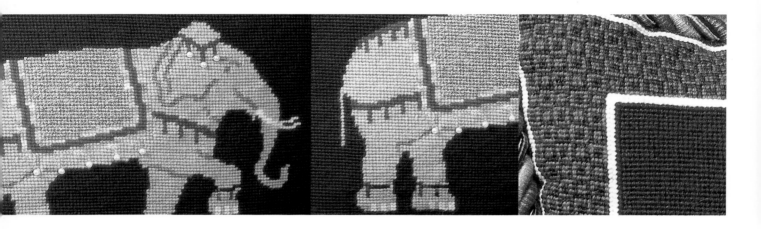

AFRICAN ELEPHANT CUSHION

MATERIALS

- 1 skein tapisserie wool 8492 and 9638
- 2 skeins tapisserie wool 9634
- 4 skeins tapisserie wool 9008,
  9560, 8006
- 5 skeins tapisserie wool 9602
- 1 skein Sunshine Pearl Cotton
- 1 skein Harlequin Pearl Cotton
- 1 reel Kreinik Heavy Braid 002
- 8 seed pearls
- 1 piece 12-hole interlock canvas size
  508mm x 406mm (20in x 16in)
- Red velvet backing fabric
- Cushion pad size 400mm x 300mm
  (15¾in x 11¾in)
- 1½m trimmings

The elephant is the largest of all land mammals and has existed for some five million years. Elephants spend most of their lives grazing and browsing in order to maintain their enormous bodies and, therefore, require a large area of land to survive. Before the lure of ivory, humans greatly admired these fascinating, complex and intelligent animals, and depicted them in every art-form.

Instructions

1 Follow the chart to work the design, starting from the middle. Use half cross-stitch throughout.

2 Press the embroidery on the back with a hot steam iron over a damp cloth and gently pull it back into shape. If it is still not straight dampen it again, pin it to a wooden board covered with a tea towel and leave to dry.

3 With right sides together, sew the backing fabric to the embroidery on three sides.

= Kreinik Heavy Braid 002

= 9638

= Sunshine Pearl Cotton

= 9560

= 8006

= 8492

= 9008

= 9634

= Harlequin Pearl Cotton

4 Trim any excess canvas to within 13mm (½in) and cut the corners diagonally.

5 Turn right sides out and insert the cushion pad.

6 Close the open seam with slip stitch.

7 Sew on trimmings.

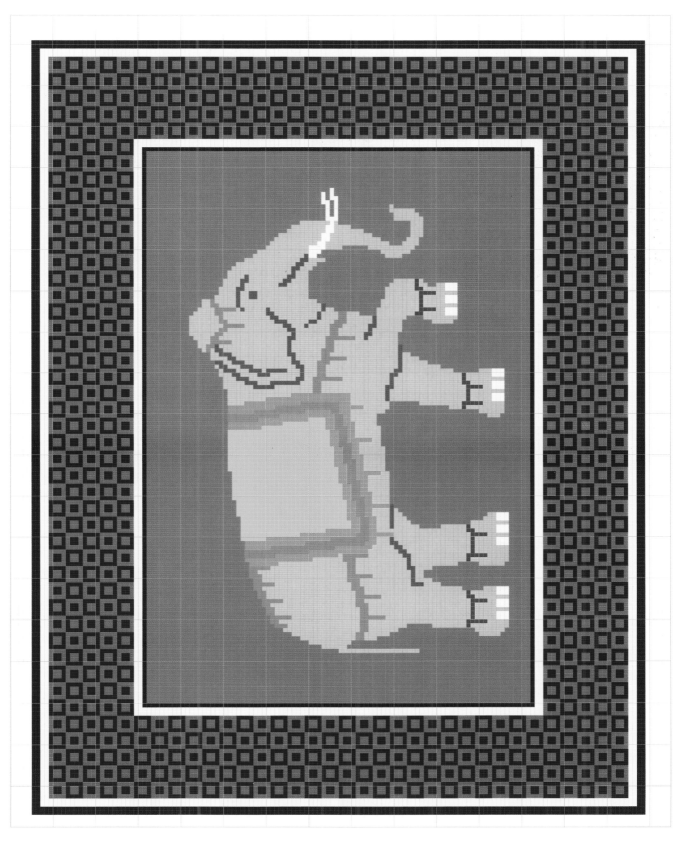

GHANAIAN PINCUSHIONS

MATERIALS

To stitch all three pincushions you will
  need the following amount of
  tapisserie wool:

- 1 skein 9022
- 2 skeins 9642, 8242, 9006, 8690
- 3 skeins 8156, 8124
- 6 pieces 12-hole interlock canvas size
  152mm (6in) square
- Stuffing

These designs were all taken from a long narrow woven piece of
fabric. Traditionally these pieces of fabric were hand-woven
over a long period of time and were used in wedding
ceremonies. Three pincushions have been made here from the
designs within the fabric and you can easily mix and match
them or use all six panels as a cushion front.

Instructions

1 Follow the charts to work the designs, starting from the
middle. Use half cross stitch throughout.

2 Press the embroideries on the back with a hot steam iron
over a damp cloth and gently pull them back into shape.

3 Trim any excess canvas to within 13mm (½in) and cut the
corners diagonally.

4 Fold the unworked canvas to the wrong side all the
way around.

■	= 8242
■	= 9006
■	= 8156
■	= 8124
■	= 9646
■	= 9002
■	= 8690
■	= 9046

5 With wrong sides facing, join the two pieces using a long-armed cross stitch starting just before one corner. Leave a 51mm (2in) gap.

6 Stuff the pincushion and stitch the gap.

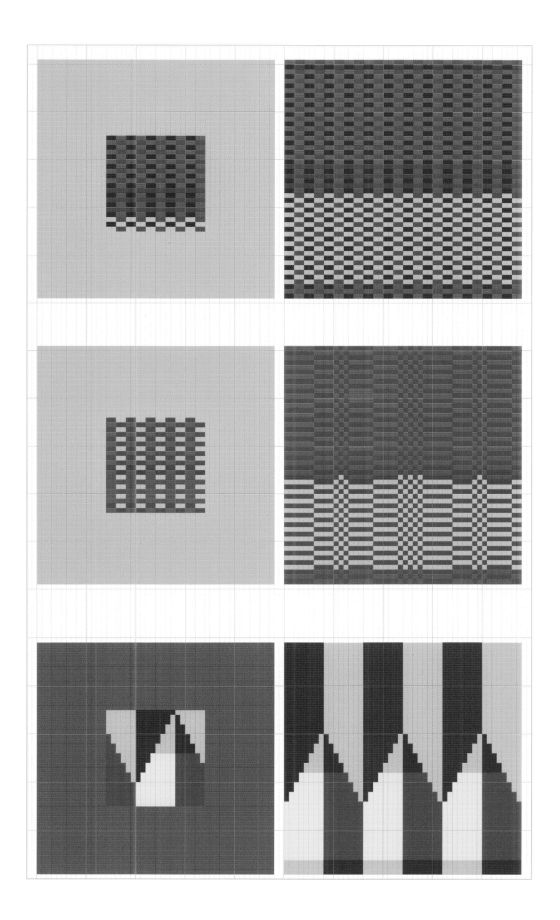

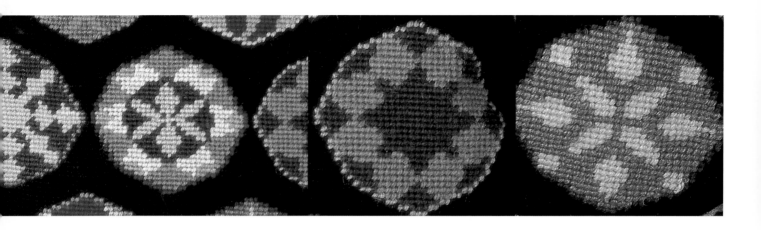

SWAZILAND ROUND CUSHION

MATERIALS

- 1 skein tapisserie wool each of: 8434, 8590, 8404, 9638, 9100, 9642, 9632, 9556, 8488
- 3 skeins tapisserie wool 9800
- 1 piece 12-hole interlock canvas size 381mm (15in) square
- Black velvet backing fabric
- 1m trimmings
- Stuffing

This cushion is based on the dyed sisal bundle-coiled baskets made in Swaziland by women using abstract patterns inspired by the world around them, such as flights of birds and activities of rural life. Generally, many basket-makers are no longer producing so much for their own use but are selling their work to the people of industrialized countries who value the natural colours and textures of traditional baskets.

Instructions

1 Follow the chart to work the design, starting from the middle. Use half cross stitch throughout.

2 Press the embroidery on the back with a hot steam iron over a damp cloth and gently pull it back into shape. If it is still not straight, dampen it again, pin it to a wooden board covered with a tea towel and leave to dry.

■	= 9800
■	= 8488
■	= 9638
■	= 8404
■	= 8434
■	= 8590
■	= 9100
■	= 9632
■	= 9556
■	= 9642

3 Trim any excess canvas to within 13mm (½in).

4 Place the embroidery and velvet backing together, right sides facing, and stitch round leaving a 152mm (6in) gap.

5 Insert the stuffing and close the gap with slip stitches.

6 Sew on the trimmings.

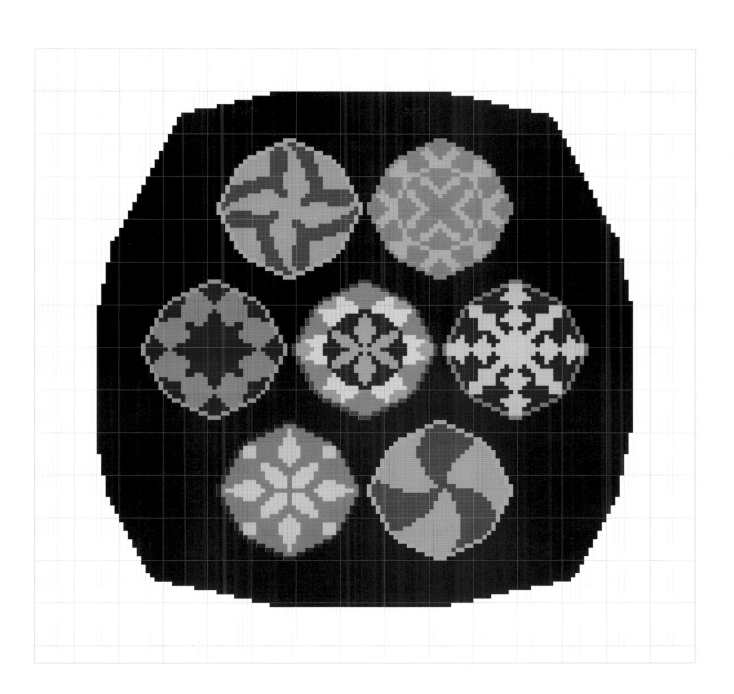

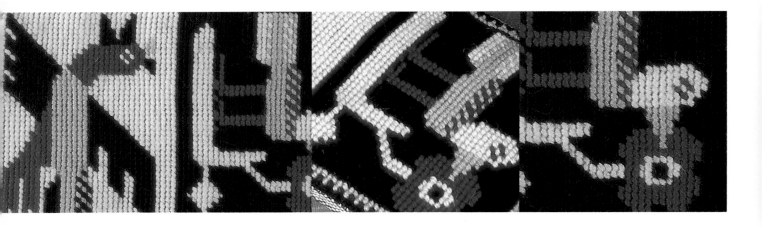

TWO BIRDS SPECTACLES CASE

MATERIALS

- 1 skein tapisserie wool 8404, 9672, 9524, 9442, 9800
- 1 piece 12-hole interlock canvas size 203mm x 305mm (8in x 12in)
- Dark red velvet backing fabric
- 2 pieces of lining fabric

Due to the differences of climate throughout Africa there are an incredible amount of birds either living there or migrating to the continent during the year. The two birds here have been stylised and were originally woven as a rug which I have adapted and used for this spectacles case design.

Instructions

1 Follow the chart to work the design, starting from the middle. Use half cross stitch throughout.

2 Press the embroidery on the back with a hot steam iron over a damp cloth and gently pull it back into shape.

3 Trim any excess canvas to within 13mm (½in) and cut the corners diagonally.

Grimm's Fai

Klee FISHER

BERTY DESIGN

BARBARA MORRIS

= 9672	
= 9442	
= 8404	
= 9524	
= 9800	
= 8402	

4 With right sides together, sew the backing fabric to the embroidery, leaving the top end open. Turn right sides out.

5 With right sides together, sew the lining fabric together leaving the top end open.

6 Put the lining inside the spectacles case and carefully sew around the open end, hiding any unworked canvas.

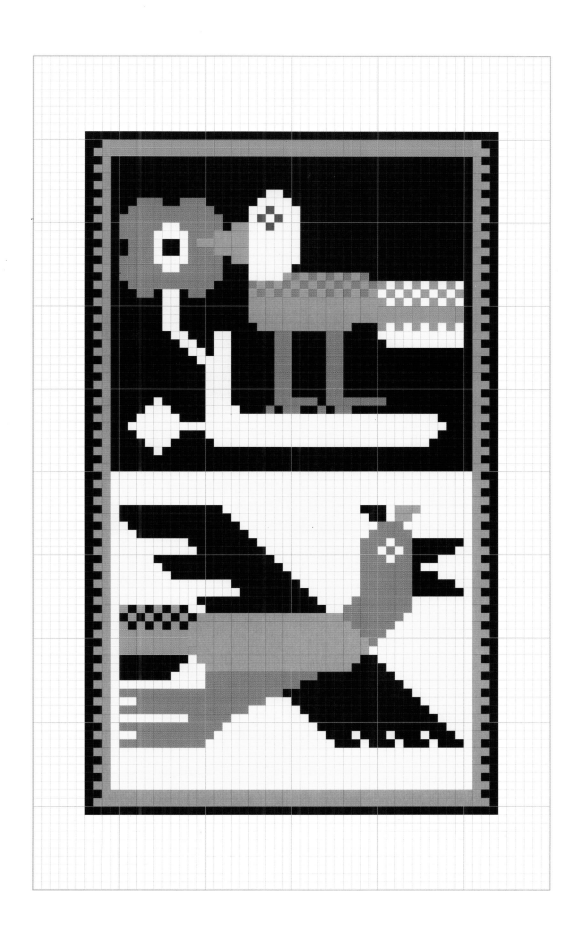

NORTH AND SOU

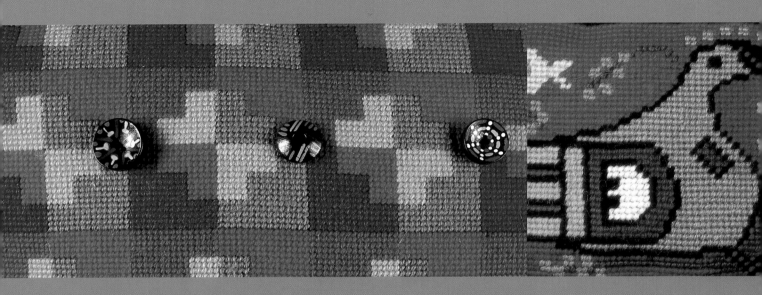

North Americans are well known for their quilt making and their embroidered samplers. But a rich supply of decorative needlework was produced by the Native Americans. Probably the earliest and most famous is quill embroidery – the application of porcupine quills to tanned leathers or birch bark. This form of decorative art was noted by the early travellers to North America.

The work was not confined to one tribe or nation but was practised throughout the woodland regions of the continent and among the Plains tribes, the Menominee tribe in the north, the Sioux and Chippewa tribes in the region of the Great Lakes and extending into Canada with the tribes along the Mackenzie River. Ceremonial and ordinary items of clothing and accessories that included shirts, moccasins, leggings, knife sheaths, medicine bags and pouches, were all

TH AMERICA

decorated with this technique. Beads were sometimes added to quill-work and gradually they became the more popular type of decoration.

In Central and South America the one commonality that holds true for native art is its function. Objects and textiles were made for religious or ritual purposes, for practical use or for personal adornment. South American textiles are another area of high artistic achievement. Inca weavers knew practically every technique known to the modern textile manufacturer and many of their works are unsurpassed in quality and beauty.

Inca textiles were woven by women using small backdrop looms. The process of weaving was a religious function, especially when the cloths were to be used as grave offerings and for wrapping the dead. The textiles reveal the vigour of their design, their glowing colours and free use of stylized geometric motifs. Warriors, animals, fish and birds are common Inca textile subjects.

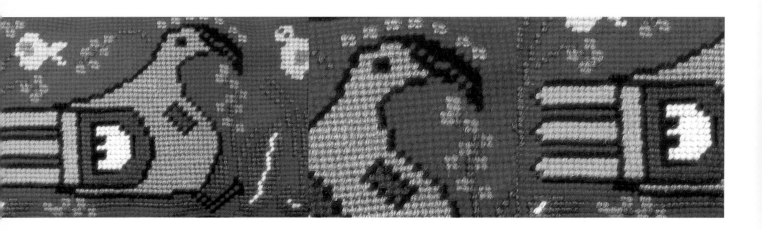

NATIVE AMERICAN SPECTACLES CASE

MATERIALS

- 1 skein each of: 9556, 8136, 8006, 9510, 8264, 9800, 8038, 9006
- 2 skeins 8218
- 1 piece 12-hole interlock canvas size 203mm x 305mm (8in x 12in)
- Black velvet backing fabric
- 2 pieces of lining fabric
- ½m red-beaded trimmings

Although the different tribes had lifestyles that ranged from secondary agriculture to nomadic hunting and gathering, all of them were profoundly influenced by the endless semi-desert landscapes of the south-west which showed through in their designs on blankets, pots and baskets. The design here depicts an eagle, which was sacred to virtually all Native American tribes.

Instructions

1 Follow the chart to work the design, starting from the middle. Use half cross stitch throughout.

2 Press the embroidery on the back with a hot steam iron over a damp cloth and gently pull it back into shape.

3 Trim any excess canvas to within 13mm (½in) and cut the corners diagonally.

4 With right sides together, sew the backing fabric to the embroidery leaving the top end open. Turn right sides out.

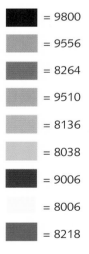

= 9800
= 9556
= 8264
= 9510
= 8136
= 8038
= 9006
= 8006
= 8218

5 With right sides together, sew the lining fabric together leaving the top end open.

6 Put the lining inside the spectacles case and carefully sew around the open end hiding any unworked canvas.

7 Carefully sew the beaded trimming around three sides.

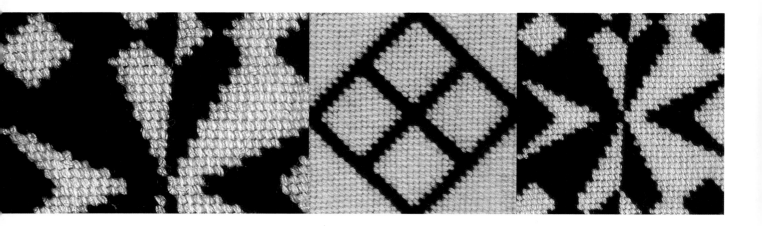

INUIT NEEDLECASE

MATERIALS

- 1 skein 8000 and 9800
- 2 pieces 12-hole interlock canvas size 178mm (7in) square
- 2 pieces lining fabric
- 1 piece of felt

The Inuits are the most widely dispersed group in the world, living in a region that spans more than 3500 miles, including North America, Greenland and a sector of eastern Siberia. The traditional dress of the Inuit people is heavy fur clothing that is simply decorated with basic geometric patterns in contrasting colours.

Instructions

1 Follow the charts to work the designs, starting from the middle. Use half cross stitch throughout.

2 Press the embroideries on the back with a hot steam iron over a damp cloth and gently pull them back into shape.

3 Trim any excess canvas to within 13mm (½in). Also cut the corners diagonally.

4 Turn the unworked canvas to the back of each embroidery, place the lining fabric over the back and slip stitch around the edge.

<table>
<tr><td>■</td><td>9800</td></tr>
<tr><td></td><td>8000</td></tr>
</table>

5 With wrong sides together, join the left-hand seam with a long-armed cross stitch.

6 Neatly sew a piece of felt down the centre seam inside.

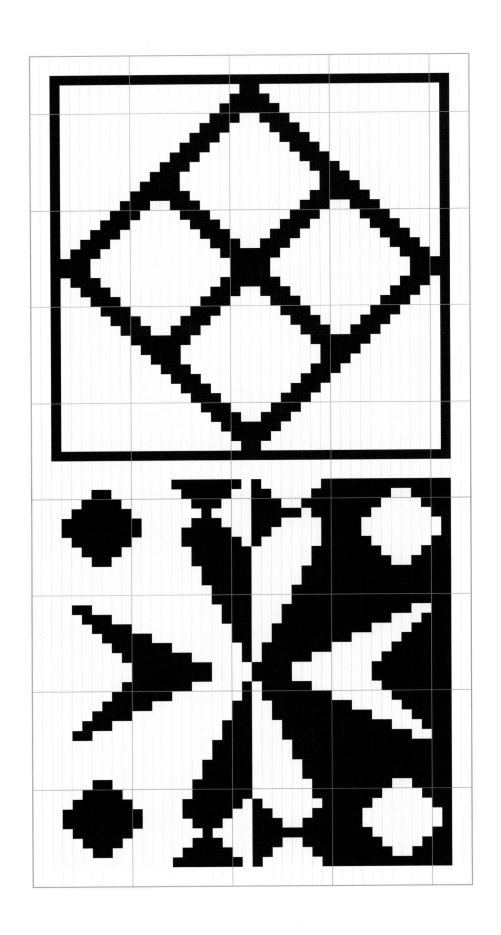

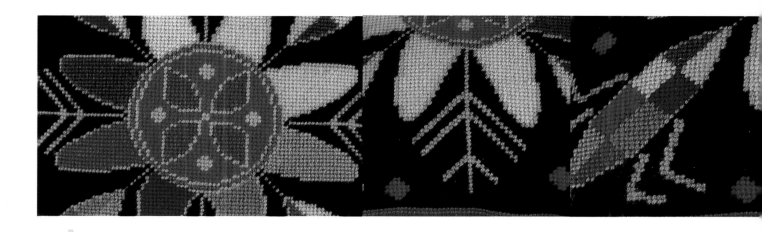

MEXICAN CUSHION

MATERIALS

- 2 skeins each of: 8038, 8218, 8452, 8134, 8432, 8688, 8690, 8734, 8590, 9006, 9098
- 4 skeins 9800
- 1 piece of 12-hole interlock canvas size 457mm (18in) square
- Black velvet backing fabric
- Cushion pad size 350mm (13¾in) square

This design was inspired from the *cuadros de estambre* or yarn pictures of the Huichol people of Mexico. These were an indigenous people who represented their spiritual ideas in yarn pictures. The themes and significance of their concepts of gods, shamans, the ceremonial use of peyote and its five associated colours are depicted in an abstract stylized manner.

Instructions

1 Follow the chart to work the design, starting from the middle. Use half cross stitch throughout.

2 Press the embroidery on the back with a hot steam iron over a damp cloth and gently pull it back into shape. If it is still not straight dampen it again, pin it to a wooden board covered with a tea towel and leave to dry.

3 With right sides together, sew the backing fabric to the embroidery on three sides.

■	= 8590
■	= 8690
▫	= 8734
▫	= 8452
■	= 8218
■	= 9098
▫	= 8038
▫	= 8134
■	= 8688
■	= 9006
▫	= 8432
■	= 9800

4 Trim any excess canvas to within 13mm (½in) and cut the corners diagonally.

5 Turn right sides out and insert the cushion pad.

6 Close the open seam with slip stitch.

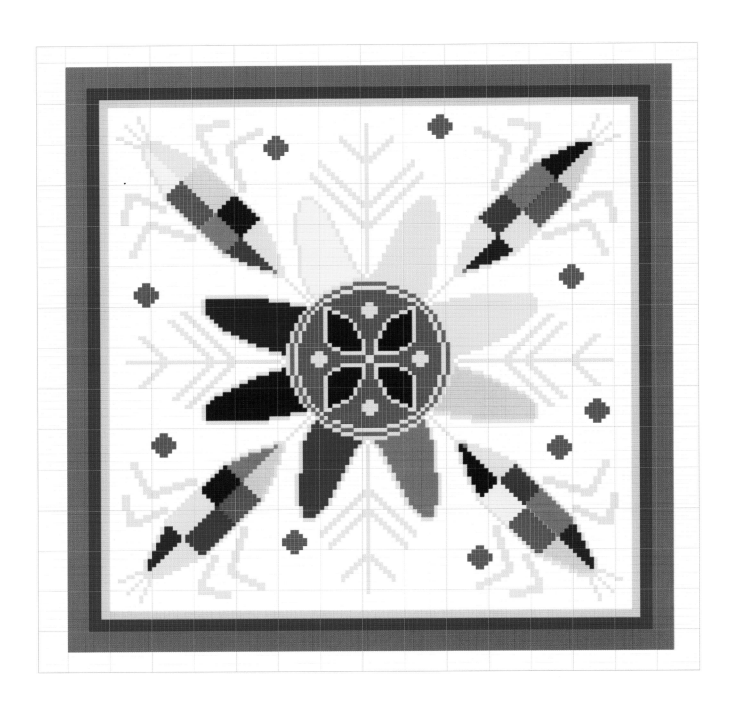

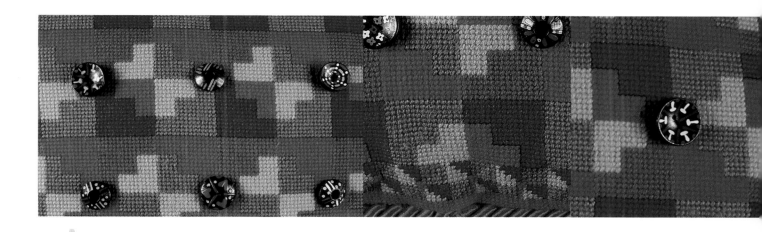

AZTEC CUSHION

MATERIALS

- 4 skeins tapisserie wool 8690, 9116, 8490, 8434
- 6 skeins tapisserie wool 8202
- 1 piece 12-hole interlock canvas size 508mm (20in) square
- Black velvet backing fabric
- Cushion pad size 450mm (17¾in) square
- 2m cord trimming
- 9 buttons

The South Central region of present-day Mexico was once the home of the Aztecs who began to settle there in the early fourteenth century. Although better known for their human sacrifices than their textiles, the ancient Aztec people greatly valued superior work and craftsmanship. This is reflected in their architecture, especially in their religious buildings, which had a vast amount of steps leading up to the top temple. It is these steps, or 'ziggurat' shapes, that I have used here in the vibrant colours of a hot climate.

Instructions

1 Follow the chart to work the design, starting from the middle. Use half cross stitch throughout.

2 Press the embroidery on the back with a hot steam iron over a damp cloth and gently pull it back into shape. If it is still not straight dampen it again, pin it to a wooden board covered with a tea towel and leave to dry.

![colour]	= 8202
![colour]	= 9116
![colour]	= 8490
![colour]	= 8434
![colour]	= 8690

3 With right sides together, sew the backing fabric to the embroidery on three sides.

4 Trim any excess canvas to within 13mm (½in) and cut the corners diagonally.

5 Turn right sides out and insert the cushion pad.

6 Close the open seam with slip stitch.

7 Sew on trimmings.

8 Sew on buttons.

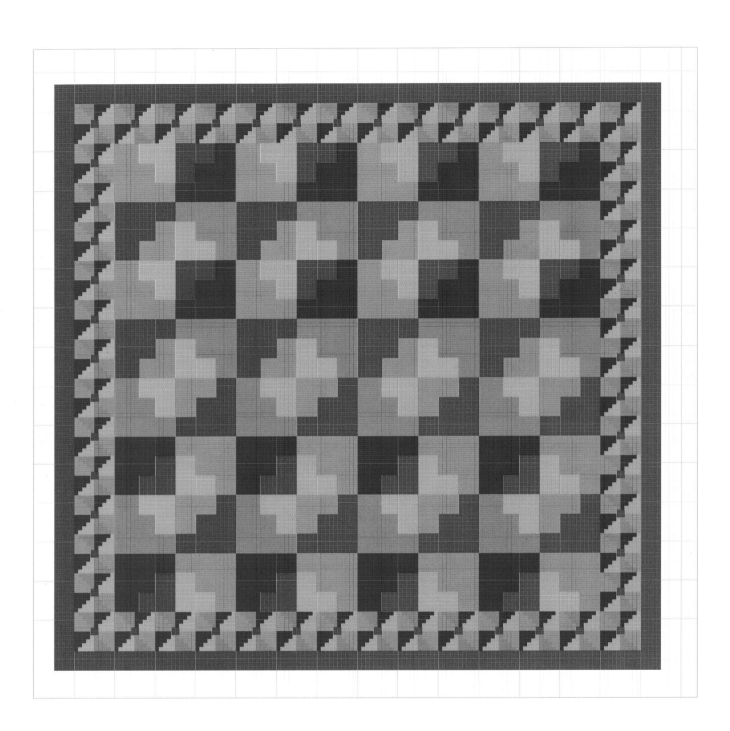

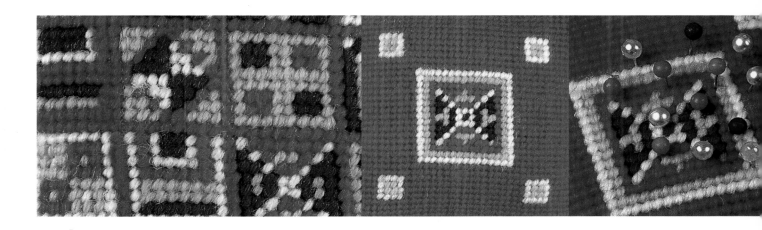

Peruvian Pincushion

MATERIALS

- 1 skein tapisserie wool 8138, 8006
- 2 skeins tapisserie wool 8690, 8216
- 2 pieces 12-hole interlock canvas size 152mm (6in) square
- Stuffing

In ancient Peru, the finest textiles were valued more highly than gold. Textiles were often buried with the dead, not just as clothing, but also as beautifully patterned lengths of cloth to wrap around the mummified body. The most spectacular designs were those made by the Paracas people for use as burial cloths. These cloths had alternating plain and embroidered squares with no two patterns ever being exactly the same. It has been estimated that each cloth took up to 30 years to complete and the patterns probably related to the dead person's status in life.

Instructions

1 Follow the chart to work the design, starting from the middle. Use half cross stitch throughout.

2 Press the embroideries on the back with a hot steam iron over a damp cloth and gently pull back into shape.

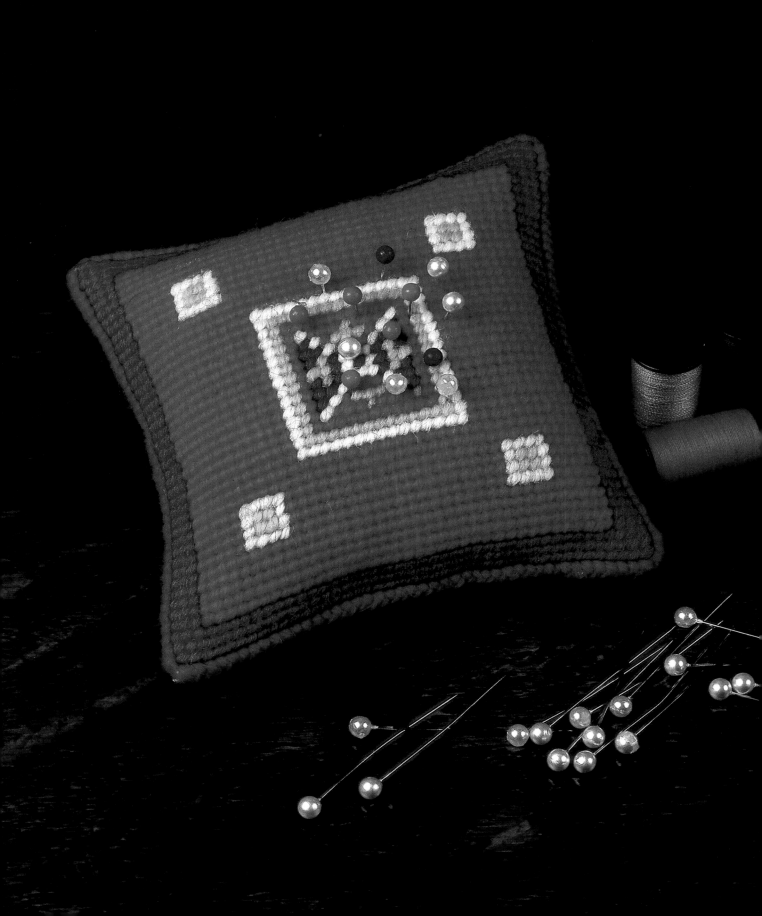

▨	= 8216
▨	= 8690
▨	= 8138
	= 8006

3 Trim any excess canvas to within 13mm (½in) and cut the corners diagonally.

4 With wrong sides facing, sew the two pieces together with a long-armed cross stitch. Leave a 51mm (2in) gap.

5 Stuff the pincushion.

6 Sew up the gap.

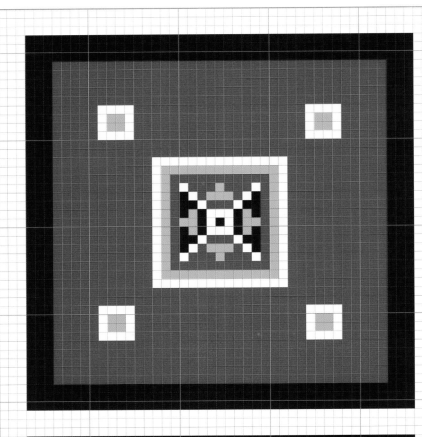

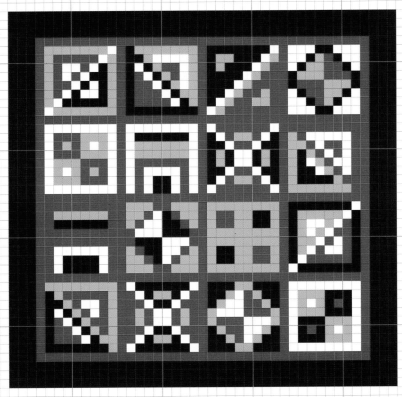

GUATEMALAN NAPKIN RINGS

MATERIALS

- 2 skeins each of stranded cotton 241, 244, 137, 363, 2, 133, 137
- 3 skeins each of stranded cotton 46, 62
- 4 pieces 14-hole interlock canvas size 305mm x 152mm (12in x 6in)
- 4 pieces pink silk backing fabric

The weavings of Guatemala have the distinct motifs and colours of each weaver's village, creating spectacular splashes of colour at the local markets. These little napkin rings have been inspired by the patterns found in a brocaded 'huipil' or woman's blouse. I have stitched them in stranded cotton to make the designs more vibrant.

Instructions

1 Follow the charts to work the designs, starting from the middle. Use half cross stitch throughout.

2 Press the embroideries on the back with a hot steam iron over a damp cloth and gently pull them back into shape.

3 Trim any excess canvas to within 13mm (½in). Also cut the corners diagonally.

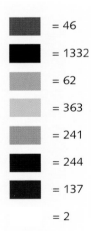

= 46	
= 1332	
= 62	
= 363	
= 241	
= 244	
= 137	
= 2	

4 Back each piece of embroidery with the silk fabric.

5 Stitch the short ends together with a long-armed cross stitch.

ABOUT THE AUTHOR

Stella Knight studied textile design at university and after working for several textile companies began to run her own needlepoint kit business. She designed and sold cushion and pincushion kits and also invented the 'leather bag kit', which soon developed to incorporate spectacles cases with a leather trim and mini purses. These were sold throughout the UK including prestigious stores such as Liberty of Regent Street, Selfridges and Harrods. The kits were also sold abroad, especially to America, Australia and Japan.

Stella has also produced exclusive designs for many magazines and has written several needlepoint and cross-stitch books. This is her seventh book. She now lives in Gloucestershire with her husband and two children where she divides her time between designing needlepoint and running a self-catering holiday cottage business.

INDEX

UPHOLSTERY

The Upholsterer's Pocket Reference Book — *David James*
Upholstery: A Complete Course (Revised Edition) — *David James*
Upholstery Restoration — *David James*
Upholstery Techniques & Projects — *David James*
Upholstery Tips and Hints — *David James*

TOYMAKING

Scrollsaw Toy Projects — *Ivor Carlyle*
Scrollsaw Toys for All Ages — *Ivor Carlyle*

DOLLS' HOUSES AND MINIATURES

1/12 Scale Character Figures for the Dolls' House — *James Carrington*
Americana in 1/12 Scale: 50 Authentic Projects — *Joanne Ogreenc & Mary Lou Santovec*
Architecture for Dolls' Houses — *Joyce Percival*
The Authentic Georgian Dolls' House — *Brian Long*
A Beginners' Guide to the Dolls' House Hobby — *Jean Nisbett*
Celtic, Medieval and Tudor Wall Hangings in 1/12 Scale Needlepoint — *Sandra Whitehead*
Creating Decorative Fabrics: Projects in 1/12 Scale — *Janet Storey*
The Dolls' House 1/24 Scale: A Complete Introduction — *Jean Nisbett*
Dolls' House Accessories, Fixtures and Fittings — *Andrea Barham*
Dolls' House Furniture: Easy-to-Make Projects in 1/12 Scale — *Freida Gray*
Dolls' House Makeovers — *Jean Nisbett*
Dolls' House Window Treatments — *Eve Harwood*
Easy to Make Dolls' House Accessories — *Andrea Barham*
Edwardian-Style Hand-Knitted Fashion for 1/12 Scale Dolls — *Yvonne Wakefield*
How to Make Your Dolls' House Special: Fresh Ideas for Decorating — *Beryl Armstrong*
Make Your Own Dolls' House Furniture — *Maurice Harper*
Making Dolls' House Furniture — *Patricia King*
Making Georgian Dolls' Houses — *Derek Rowbottom*
Making Miniature Chinese Rugs and Carpets — *Carol Phillipson*
Making Miniature Food and Market Stalls — *Angie Scarr*
Making Miniature Gardens — *Freida Gray*
Making Miniature Oriental Rugs & Carpets — *Meik & Ian McNaughton*
Making Period Dolls' House Accessories — *Andrea Barham*
Making Tudor Dolls' Houses — *Derek Rowbottom*
Making Victorian Dolls' House Furniture — *Patricia King*
Medieval and Tudor Needlecraft: Knights and Ladies in 1/12 Scale — *Sandra Whitehead*
Miniature Bobbin Lace — *Roz Snowden*
Miniature Embroidery for the Georgian Dolls' House — *Pamela Warner*
Miniature Embroidery for the Tudor and Stuart Dolls' House — *Pamela Warner*
Miniature Embroidery for the Victorian Dolls' House — *Pamela Warner*
Miniature Needlepoint Carpets — *Janet Granger*
More Miniature Oriental Rugs & Carpets — *Meik & Ian McNaughton*
Needlepoint 1/12 Scale: Design Collections for the Dolls' House — *Felicity Price*
New Ideas for Miniature Bobbin Lace — *Roz Snowden*
Patchwork for the Dolls' House: 20 Projects in 1/12 Scale — *Sarah Williams*

CRAFTS

American Patchwork Designs in Needlepoint — *Melanie Tacon*
Bargello: A Fresh Approach to Florentine Embroidery — *Brenda Day*
Beginning Picture Marquetry — *Lawrence Threadgold*
Blackwork: A New Approach — *Brenda Day*
Celtic Cross Stitch Designs — *Carol Phillipson*
Celtic Knotwork Designs — *Sheila Sturrock*
Celtic Knotwork Handbook — *Sheila Sturrock*
Celtic Spirals and Other Designs — *Sheila Sturrock*
Complete Pyrography — *Stephen Poole*
Creating Made-to-Measure Knitwear: A Revolutionary Approach to Knitwear Design — *Sylvia Wynn*
Creative Backstitch — *Helen Hall*
Creative Embroidery Techniques Using Colour Through Gold — *Daphne J. Ashby & Jackie Woolsey*
The Creative Quilter: Techniques and Projects — *Pauline Brown*
Cross-Stitch Designs from China — *Carol Phillipson*
Decoration on Fabric: A Sourcebook of Ideas — *Pauline Brown*
Decorative Beaded Purses — *Enid Taylor*
Designing and Making Cards — *Glennis Gilruth*
Glass Engraving Pattern Book — *John Everett*
Glass Painting — *Emma Sedman*
Handcrafted Rugs — *Sandra Hardy*
How to Arrange Flowers: A Japanese Approach to English Design — *Taeko Marvelly*
How to Make First-Class Cards — *Debbie Brown*
An Introduction to Crewel Embroidery — *Mave Glenny*
Making and Using Working Drawings for Realistic Model Animals — *Basil F. Fordham*
Making Character Bears — *Valerie Tyler*
Making Decorative Screens — *Amanda Howes*
Making Fabergé-Style Eggs — *Denise Hopper*
Making Fairies and Fantastical Creatures — *Julie Sharp*
Making Greetings Cards for Beginners — *Pat Sutherland*
Making Hand-Sewn Boxes: Techniques and Projects — *Jackie Woolsey*
Making Mini Cards, Gift Tags & Invitations — *Glennis Gilruth*
Making Soft-Bodied Dough Characters — *Patricia Hughes*
Natural Ideas for Christmas: Fantastic Decorations to Make — *Josie Cameron-Ashcroft & Carol Cox*
New Ideas for Crochet: Stylish Projects for the Home — *Darsha Capaldi*
Papercraft Projects for Special Occasions — *Sine Chesterman*
Patchwork for Beginners — *Pauline Brown*
Pyrography Designs — *Norma Gregory*
Pyrography Handbook (Practical Crafts) — *Stephen Poole*
Rose Windows for Quilters — *Angela Besley*
Rubber Stamping with Other Crafts — *Lynne Garner*
Silk Painting — *Jill Clay*
Sponge Painting — *Ann Rooney*
Stained Glass: Techniques and Projects — *Mary Shanahan*
Step-by-Step Pyrography Projects for the Solid Point Machine — *Norma Gregory*
Tassel Making for Beginners — *Enid Taylor*
Tatting Collage — *Lindsay Rogers*
Tatting Patterns — *Lyn Morton*
Temari: A Traditional Japanese Embroidery Technique — *Margaret Ludlow*
Trip Around the World: 25 Patchwork, Quilting and Appliqué Projects — *Gail Lawther*
Trompe l'Oeil: Techniques and Projects — *Jan Lee Johnson*
Tudor Treasures to Embroider — *Pamela Warner*
Wax Art — *Hazel Marsh*

GARDENING

Alpine Gardening — *Chris & Valerie Wheeler*
Auriculas for Everyone: How to Grow and Show Perfect Plants — *Mary Robinson*
Beginners' Guide to Herb Gardening — *Yvonne Cuthbertson*
Beginners' Guide to Water Gardening — *Graham Clarke*
Bird Boxes and Feeders for the Garden — *Dave Mackenzie*
The Birdwatcher's Garden — *Hazel & Pamela Johnson*
Broad-Leaved Evergreens — *Stephen G. Haw*

PHOTOGRAPHY

ART TECHNIQUES

VIDEOS

MAGAZINES

WOODTURNING ◆ WOODCARVING ◆ FURNITURE & CABINETMAKING
THE ROUTER ◆ NEW WOODWORKING ◆ THE DOLLS' HOUSE MAGAZINE
OUTDOOR PHOTOGRAPHY ◆ BLACK & WHITE PHOTOGRAPHY
TRAVEL PHOTOGRAPHY
MACHINE KNITTING NEWS ◆ BUSINESSMATTERS

The above represents a full list of all titles currently published or scheduled to be published.
All are available direct from the Publishers or through bookshops, newsagents and specialist retailers.
To place an order, or to obtain a complete catalogue, contact:

GMC Publications,
Castle Place, 166 High Street, Lewes, East Sussex BN7 1XU, United Kingdom
Tel: 01273 488005 Fax: 01273 478606
E-mail: pubs@thegmcgroup.com

Orders by credit card are accepted